Forward

I am a dentist, a dental coach and a consultant. I am writing this book primarily for dentists and other dental consultants who work within this industry. Because of that, many of my references may be a little confusing to non-dental folks. I make no apology for this. The intent of this book is to help the dental community increase their Emotional Intelligence, which will result in them being more successful and happy in their chosen profession.

And now, a brief disclaimer: I have recently retired after 45 years of clinical dental practice, and I come from an age there there was only one woman in my dental class. It's also worth noting that the town I moved to when I started my practice had no women dentists. While I believe that women make excellent dentists, when I write, I have a hard time writing in a "gender neutral" way. There is no malice intended, but you will see a lot of "he's" and very few "they's" and "she's." I hope there is no offense taken by this.

I have borrowed from many works and authors, but the basic points all originally come from "Emotional Intelligence," the seminal work of Daniel Goleman. It is hard to make up new classifications or names used to describe the skills he originally used, so I did not try to change those, and give him credit for these characteristics and names. After reading that book, I noticed that many other works about Emotional Intelligence use the same language, and I did not see the point in trying to remake the wheel. I have included a bibliography of the books I read in preparation for writing this book should you be interested in exploring this subject in greater depth.

Biography

Drawing from 40+ years of clinical experience practicing in a small suburban blue collar town – as well as Pankey-Dawson clinical training, Dr. David Black helps dentists and their teams increase profitability, patient standard of care and peace of mind through attention to key systems.

A dental leader in local societies and projects, and state dental board of directors, committees and task forces, Dr. Black's proven leadership and administrative skill were fundamental in developing a successful restorative and cosmetic practice. Over the years Dr. Black has hired and mentored dozens of dentists, proven his systems for creating a highly-profitable, low-overhead business model, and provided outstanding patient care.

Dr. Black's interest in Emotional Intelligence has come from a natural extension of his consulting experiences and his interest in Leadership in the dental office. After study of Personality Types in DiSC studies by Wiley Co and Pat Lencioni's "Five Dysfunctions of a Team", the natural progression was why are some bosses better leaders than others. Dr. Black was led to the seminal work on the subject, "Emotional Intelligence", by Goleman and also to a related work, "Sales EQ", by Blount. Dr. Black thought this same information could be applied to dentistry and how dental Leaders who are successful apply their EQ to their relationships and their business. You can find shorter e-books on subjects of dental transitions on his Website- Pinpoint Dental Consulting.

Table of Contents

Dentistry And Emotional Intelligence 2

IQ Or EQ, What Is The Difference? 8

Five Skills That Are The Hallmarks Of Emotional Intelligence .. 14

How EQ Applies To Dentistry.............................. 24

Which Personality Traits Are Affected By EQ &
How Do They Apply To Dentistry?......................... 28

Symptoms Of Low EQ 38

How Low Dental EQ Affects Your Practice 42

How To Improve Your Emotional Intelligence 48

Dental Behavior That Is Outdated And
Does Not Express High EQ 66

Exercises You Can Use To Improve Your Emotional Intelligence 70

Does Emotional Intelligence Improve With Age? 74

Benefits to Raising Your EQ.............................. 76

The Last Word 82

Bibliography 84

Dentistry and Emotional Intelligence

The Difference Between Good Leaders and Great Leaders

I have been a dentist for over 45 years. I have learned from some of the most respected dentists in the last 50 years. When I think of great dentists, the first one I think of is Dr. L.D. Pankey. He practiced in south Florida for many years and was so well thought of, the L.D. Pankey Institute in Key Biscayne, Florida was named after him. I attended classes there during five different weeks in the mid-seventies and had the distinct pleasure of meeting and learning from Dr. Pankey himself. His name is synonymous with excellence in dentistry and what he called a Philosophy of Practice. He started a study club that investigated how to do complex dental cases in a predictable way and how to teach this repeatable system to other dentists. He had his study group perform an analysis and was able to develop not only how they were going to perform the process, but also the "Why" behind it. Part of his Philosophy also included the Cross of Life, which placed an emphasis on the need to balance Work, Play, Worship and Love. Love, the fourth arm of the cross, refers to having emotional health.

The great dentists of the world all have the required technical and analytical skills; they can figure out how to repair and restore complicated situations. They can write books and teach classes that help the rest of us mortals learn part of what they know. But the best dentists can take their craft to a new level using Emotional

Intelligence, which is the emotional portion of a person's makeup that sets them apart, that allows them to look at things differently. They can look at themselves and others and understand what is going on the inside of their brain. They can then reach out to others and help them become intellectually and emotionally better.

All leaders have three skill sets in differing degrees: Operational skills, Cognitive skills, and Emotional Intelligence. All are necessary to be a great leader, and everyone have varying amounts of each skill. The more refined each of these skills, the better leader a person will be.

> <u>Operational skills</u> are purely technical skills, like clinical competence, or what we often call "good hands," as well as business savvy.

This is a baseline requirement. It is often said that dentistry is an art and a science, but often overlooked is the fact that you have to be technically excellent to be a good dentist. One of the smartest students in our freshman class had such poor technical skills, I remember him quitting our dental class near the end of our first semester when an instructor looked at his wax-up of a practice denture set-up and told him that it was not acceptable and he needed to do a lot of work to make it right. The student looked at the wax-up, walked over to the trashcan in the laboratory, and threw the project into the trash. He then walked down the hall to the Dean's office, where he withdrew from dental school then and there.

Business acumen, or the ability to run a business well, is something that gets very little attention in dental school because of material of a clinical type that demands so much time. These days, many schools are giving more attention to this side of the business, as well as seminars offered by doctors to help provide students with the information that they will need when they graduate in order for them to navigate this part of the profession. For more information about the things a new doctor needs to do when setting up a business, download my Beginner's Guide E-Book, available on the resources page of my website: Pinpoint-Dental.com/resources.

Cognitive abilities, like analytical reasoning, are used in diagnosis and planning treatment. Once again there are two separate skill sets here.

First is the analytical reasoning we use in all our business and interpersonal interactions. Our business requires us to make rational decisions every day. We have to be able to gather, sort through and analyze our decisions across multiple disciplines every day. The ability to do this is essential to staying in business and avoiding lawsuits.

The skill is in our gathering clinical information for needed treatment on our patients, sorting through all the treatment choices, deciding what is right and wrong, and what are the best choices for the patient. We then have to be able to convey our diagnosis to the patient in a way that is easy for them to digest so that they can make the best choice of treatment for their particular circumstances.

Emotional intelligence is the ability to work with others and be effective in leading change. This third quality is the one major attribute that is crucial to being a succesful leader. It is the ability to understand the emotions you are feeling, be reflective and mindful of what is going on in your mind. It is being able to recognize those same feelings and emotions in other people, and learning how to manage your relationship with those other people by applying these skills. It also involves learning social skills to get along with others, and having a conviction and a drive to work with others in a successful way.

What I am going to cover in this book is that third capability: Emotional Intelligence, or EQ. There are hundreds of books and classes on the technical, clinical skills. There are hundreds of books on how to run a successful business and improve your cognitive abilities.

But there has been very little written about how Emotional Intelligence in Dentistry is an essential skill and, more specifically, how this skill is as important to setting you apart as an exceptional dentist instead of simply a skilled clinical dentist that never quite makes it to the that next level. This book will help you learn how to attain the skills to move your game to the elite level you hope for.

The Basics of Emotional Intelligence

What is Emotion?

Emotion can be defined as a feeling and its distinctive thoughts, along with the psychological and biological states related to the feeling, and the range of actions you may desire to take related to these feelings.

Our emotional mind is much quicker to act than our rational mind. The emotional mind will jump on a situation and deliver the emotional, "first impulse" response to your body quicker than you can think through a situation. That is why we need to recognize what our emotional brain is doing, and intercept those emotions before we do something that may not be productive.

Some of the common emotions we feel are anger, sadness, fear, enjoyment, love, surprise, disgust, and shame, along with the thousands of variations of each one. One study shows that there are some core emotions that have recognizable facial expressions that are universally understood by most cultures across the world.

If you expand the study further outside emotions, there can be MOODS that often last longer than the knee-jerk EMOTIONAL reaction. And beyond moods are TEMPERMENTS, which are personality traits that repeat the same emotion or mood and come to define someone's behavior on a regular basis. This is usually explained as how someone typically will act and react to any set of circumstances. There are also DISORDERS which are clinical diseases that need treatment, often when emotions have become pathological and often are out of our conscious control.

We are going to discuss Emotions, and how we can recognize and control them so that we can get along better and be a better leader.

It is not that Intelligence or IQ is not important or irrelevant; in fact, most good leaders have high intelligence, but IQ is really just a "threshold capacity." It is only the starting point, a basic qualification, and the leadership ability is an entry-level requirement for executive positions, specifically being an accomplished dentist and team leader of your dental team.

Without EQ, no amount of intelligence or cognitive ability will push you into being a great leader.

What is Dental Emotional Intelligence (EQ)?

Simply put, Dental EQ is taking this new psychological science area of EQ, and looking at the specific areas in dentistry that are impacted by how well we can control our emotions, understand others, and build the social skills and motivation that enable us to become more effective in running our practices and our lives. I feel that since dentistry is a service profession, almost everything we say and do requires Dental EQ to help us to give that high level of personalized service that is essential to running a successful, thriving practice.

We will explore behaviors of people with high EQ and also discuss what low EQ looks like. We will also look at the advantages of improving your Dental EQ and some practical ways you can actually raise your Dental EQ.

IQ OR EQ, WHAT IS THE DIFFERENCE?

IQ Is Hard Wired Into Your Brain

Most studies show that our IQ is something we are born with. It is a measure of what our capacity is as a baseline and no matter what we do, and there is very little variation we can achieve by more schooling or more study.

We can gain more knowledge, and we can learn more things, but our innate capacity to learn or process information will stay at pretty much the same level throughout our life. As we get older, what seems like gaining more intellect is most likely attributed to the wisdom that comes from a variety of experiences in our lifetime. If our memory is good, we can process what we have learned and what we remember to make us seem more intelligent, but that is more a function of memory and processing the events than raw intelligence.

What is EQ?

I will explain the five core values of EQ in the next section, but EQ may be explained more simply as "common sense", or Mindfulness. It is more how you process your life experiences and how you get along with others.

In this fast paced world, we very often do not slow down enough to reflect on how our life is going, or how we are reacting emotionally to the world around us. I read a book recently on bringing more intention into our lives. For example, what do we do and what do we decide NOT to do? What do we set out to intentionally make an important part of our life, what do we focus on? Part of becoming more emotionally intelligent is bringing more intention to the experiences in our lives by deciding how to REACT to the things happening around us, what we decide to make the MOST important things in our life, and how we REACT to what other people do to us. How do we interact with our whole environment, our family, our job, the world in general? What are the decisions we need to make about our health and our lifestyle? It is these decisions and others that we must make daily about how we will live our lives.

Example: High IQ/Low EQ

I experienced a prime example of the difference between IQ and EQ during my time in dental school. It takes at least an above average IQ to get through undergraduate classes like Organic Chemistry, Human Anatomy, and Physiology with good enough grades to get accepted into dental school. The first two years of dental school cover basic sciences and introductory clinical dental skills. It takes at least 35-40 hours of instruction per week, plus the studying to keep up with testing. It is a tough environment for most of us average dental students.

Then there were students like D (I am not using his real name, so for all intents and purposes, I shall refer to him as D in this next section). D was brilliant, scholastically at the top of our class in all the basic sciences, learned quickly and had good retention of material presented. He sat in the front row of our lecture hall, and always seemed to be on the edge of his seat, listening intently to every work coming from the professor. Whenever the professor asked a question, D would quickly raise his hand, to let the professor know he had the right answer, and often would utter, "Oh! Oh! Oh! I know," much to the disgust of most of us in class. And he did this often. At first the professor would call on him, and almost always, he had the right answer, which still did not please most of the students in the room.

Eventually, the professors would look past him, to call on others. He was annoying, overbearing, and clueless about how his behavior affected most of us in the class. We all knew he was very smart, but we joked about how he would probably end up being a professor somewhere because he had such a Low EQ he would not be able to make a living if he had to have any kind of emotional connection with others. He wanted people to know how smart he was, and didn't care much about what others had to say. He didn't seem to know the effect he had on others, or not care in the case that he actually knew what others thought.

It was great for him to be smart enough to get straight "A's," but his inability to connect with his classmates and the professors, did not help his social interactions or endear him to anyone.

Leadership/EQ Connections

There are many types of Leaders including Dictators, Benevolent Dictators, Consensus Leaders, Abdicators, Passive Leaders and Charismatic Leaders.

> **Dictators** can often get things done, but they use power and force to gain their goals. They leave the bodies along the way. They often are effective for a time, but their style does not lend itself to keeping long-time staff on the team, an essential to the long-term success of a team. They quite often do not

care about the feelings of others and are very low on the empathy scale.

Benevolent Dictators are often found in dental offices. Doctors often do not want to take the time to get consensus in an office, understand the goals set forward, and mandate that all the team follow their lead as stated. On the other hand, the doctor may love the team, and wants the best for them as far as job security and enjoyment of their job, he just doesn't include asking their opinion on matters he sees as his business only.

Other types of leaders in the office include:

Consensus Leaders. They will often spend a lot of time training and asking the team about most decisions. Their personality usually prefers harmony and the attempt to avoid conflicts. They are usually not strong leaders, and may have trouble confronting uncomfortable situations, but their team will probably enjoy working with them, UNTIL there is a situation where a strong unpopular decision has to be made.

Abdicator Leaders. They will deflect as much of the decision-making as they possibly can in order to not make unpopular decisions. They will assign the dirty work to someone else on the team. They really are not strong leaders, but may be a manager instead.

Passive Leaders. Similar to the Abdicator in many ways, but the operative behavior may be more of ignoring situations and hoping they will take care of themselves or better yet, just go away. They will usually try to get everyone into a specific role, and let the practice sort of run itself.

Charismatic Leader. They may be weak or strong, but a Charismatic Leader rules mostly by their presence or personality. They are usually well liked and seen as a great leader based on how they handle people and situations. I have seen this played out in large corporations like Chrysler with Lee Iacocca and in many large churches with leaders with great speaking and interpersonal skills. In a lot of situations, when the Charismatic Leader is gone, the corporation or church relapses because it was so reliant on the personality of the leader there was no sustainable infrastructure to carry on the work.

Good Leadership can come in many different styles. There are good and bad leaders. Just because someone has risen to the top of a company does not mean they lead well. Most of us may lead well in one area and be poor in another. Will Rogers said," Everybody is ignorant, only on different subjects."

When someone has good leadership qualities, they usually have an emotionally intelligent approach to that particular area. If someone is clueless about how others react to them, they will have problems leading. If they are just mean and disrespectful, they will have poor relationships with their employee and their patients.

FIVE SKILLS THAT ARE THE HALLMARKS OF EMOTIONAL INTELLIGENCE

1. Self-Awareness
2. Self-Regulation
3. Empathy
4. Social Skill
5. Motivation

1. SELF-AWARENESS: Know Yourself

This is the MOST important step in becoming emotionally intelligent. This is also sometimes referred to as being self-reflective and mindful. In a lot of ways, this reminds me of some of the non-secular Principles of Yoga and Christian Meditation. Most of EQ revolves around this skill, and the other four competencies revolve around and build upon this skill.

Being self-reflective is harder for most of us left-brained, scientifically trained, straight-line thinkers. For us, it is just "Ready-Aim-Fire." We do not spend much time recalibrating our sights. I have found this to be an easier skill for me to embrace and practice since I have retired from clinical dentistry. All day long I went from one physical task to the next, with my brain staying busy on the job right in front of me and the mental exercises it took to deal with each moment.

Luckily, my morning devotionals that became my habit in later years, pointed me toward reflecting on what I was reading or studying that day, and quieted my mind and spirit, even for a short time each day. Applying this to how I reacted to the emotional flood of stimuli that came at me each day, kept me unconsciously practicing this reflection exercise before it became a conscious exercise. I was not analyzing my emotions, nor how that effected my interaction with others and my internal emotional and physical state in times of tension and conflict that come naturally when managing and leading a business.

There are various ways to track and monitor your emotional state, but one of the simplest is to make a note to yourself every ten minutes for a one-hour interval during the day. What emotions you are feeling at any given moment? Make note of the emotion, and then note what were the circumstances in that moment that caused you to have that emotion. You may want to do this and later reflect on the event:

- Was it positive or negative?
- Did you react appropriately or not?
- Would it be better to change your response to the feeling?
- Is this the prevailing mood or emotion you have all day long?
- How does it affect the people around you?
- If it is negative, how can you react in a different way?
- What can you change about yourself or your environment to make it more positive? Was there a specific trigger that caused the emotion?
- Did you notice any physical changes in your body during both positive and negative situations?
- Did you tense up, did you get a headache, did you break out in a sweat?
- Did your heart beat faster?

If you can do this interval once per day for one week, then reflect on it's effect on you, you have a good exercise to start the process of mindfulness. You can see how this is so important. Without this part, you will NEVER be able to move to the other three parts.

2. SELF-REGULATION: Managing Your Emotions

The first thing you must do to manage your own emotions is to decide what is an appropriate range of emotions to have for any given circumstance and to have the ability to control or redirect disruptive impulses and moods.

The second is to determine what your preferred response would be for each circumstance. This would not be something that you do by sitting down and making a detailed list when you decide you need improvement. Most likely, this would be something that is determined as each and every new circumstance comes up. This probably will not be written anywhere except in some part of your brain. That isn't to say that it wouldn't be a good idea to write some of your thoughts down as a reminder, it just usually isn't going to take place.

This is something that will happen for both positive and negative stimuli. How do you respond to a kind word? How do you react to the affection of your wife or child? How do you respond to praise? Or criticism? When do you feel fear, and how do you react?

Emotions, in brain science, are the most basic of instincts, being located in the limbic system of our brain, and it makes us have physical as well as mental and emotional responses. We will need to learn how to read our physical cues in our bodies when we have stimuli that affects us.

One of the most common responses is "fight or flight." The

body interprets this as something that is dangerous, and shifts blood flow to large muscles and away from other organs so you can protect yourself. In other words, we simply REACT.

If someone verbally attacks us, or even disagrees, the body will have a reaction that creates physical changes. This is a learned response. Part of controlling our emotions is being to able to READ our body, to know what emotion we are feeling, sorting through the consequence of this change, and interpreting how best to react to this change to end up with the best social consequence.

Most of this is learned over time, learning from the consequences of poor responses or being rewarded when we make a good response. We learn to judge our environment and how the people around us respond to what we say and do. This is where "common sense," judgment and wisdom all come into play. If we have high EQ, we will quickly learn what is our preferred outcome for each and every interaction.

In a lot of cases, we will try to stretch the outcomes in our favor, to get more of what we want. We will also learn from this what is an overreach of our desires, through negative feedback, and adapt our approach.

It can be helpful to have a retrospective look at poor management of our responses. This is the first step in self-reflection, where mindfulness steps in, and the real learning begins.

First, we must know what emotions we are actually experiencing and then decide if they are good or bad emotions to have in response to the situation. Then we have to look at our emotions through the lens of either accepting what is going on, or changing our emotions or our behavior.

When your spouse says your behavior is unacceptable, how do you respond? How do you react at work when you feel someone is acting inappropriately or doing a poor job? Do you accept it? Do you lash out? What emotions do you have in this situation? Do you consider what response you will get back? Are you ready to suffer the consequence to your relationship because of the way you respond? Do you take the part of a mediator to create peace? Do you grin and bear it, but then you have other negative emotions because of your passive stance?

This is where you have to make specific choices about your life: How do you want to live? How do you want to be perceived by others? Where do you need to take a stand?

If you are a Leader, how does this define how you lead?

3. EMPATHY: Know Other

Empathy starts with knowing yourself and the emotional range you have in your own life. You will not be able to truly understand the emotions of others until you know the range of your own emotions. Unless someone is psychotic or a sociopath, they will probably have the same range of emotions that you and your colleagues have.

But just because you know that you react a certain way, do not make the mistake of thinking that others will have the same reaction to the same stimulus that you have. You will be dealing with a full range of EQ in different people. People process their responses in their life uniquely, not necessarily in the same way that you do. A good leader will be considerate of other's feelings, especially when making decisions that also effect themselves.

Having studied DiSC personality traits and preferences, statistically only 25% of any population will react to things remotely close to the way you do. There are four distinct personality types, with thousands of hybrids within them, each unique to every individual person, so the chance of a person processing information the same ways that you do is very remote. It would be safer to assume that no one will interpret the same information the same way as you do.

The four distinct personality types as interpreted by Wiley, Inc., DiSC® personality test are <u>Dominant, Influencer, Steadiness, and Conscientiousness</u>.

> <u>Dominant</u> personalities tend to be action oriented, direct, strong-willed and forceful.
>
> <u>Influencer</u> personalities tend to be high-energy, very talkative and the center of attention.
>
> <u>Steadiness</u> personalities tend to be gentle, peaceful, accommodating and accepting. They do not like change, and are often found in the dental office in helping roles.
>
> <u>Conscientiousness</u> personalities tend to be analytical, reserved and have a strong focus on accuracy. A lot of accountants and engineers fall into this category.

Wiley breaks these four down into twelve subcategories for the purpose of looking at the hybrids of the four. All of us have elements of all four personalities, however, the way in which we respond to other people and experiences leans towards one dominant personality trait over the other three.

The best way to Know Others is to look at their response to stimuli and try to interpret if that response is appropriate given the circumstances. In the same way that you have your own set of emotions when someone responds to you, you need to become sensitive to pushback or irritation, or positive response to your interaction. Once again, this is not an innate behavior for many of us. I contend that we most often respond in our own self-interest and encounter resistance from others when we act in our own interest.

Reading how others react is a learned skill, similar to learning our physical boundaries from a bruised nose or a skinned knee. Although Knowing Yourself and developing self-awareness is the basic skill needed, in business, it is probably Knowing Others that will lead to the most success. By being a student of others, you will become a better salesperson, coach, consultant and friend. Some of this will be by trial and error, but as you practice it more, you will become better with each interaction. If you practice the first principle of knowing yourself, and how interactions make you feel, the emotions you have and how you react, will lead to knowing others. By knowing how you react, you can avoid some of the poor choices you make in talking to others and you will become a better listener, finding out how and why others are reacting as they do.

4. SOCIAL SKILLS: Manage Your Relationships

Knowing Others is the start of Managing your Relationships. The goal is to move people in the desired direction through your leadership, being persuasive and being an expert in leading teams.

Do you see how these all dovetail? How can you manage a relationship if you are clueless?

I had a dental team that stayed with me for many years. Upon my retirement, I had one employee who worked with me for 34 years and a team of 7 employees with several at or over 20 years each. I hired all of them before I knew anything about Emotional

Intelligence, but I did know how I liked to be treated with respect and to be told what was expected of me.

I ignorantly applied these principles to try to make my team happy and remain with me. I use the word Ignorant in the best possible context. I just didn't know that I was doing anything special, other than applying what my family and my hometown values had taught me. I played high school sports and I was not the most skilled, but I worked hard to be a team player, to help others, and to have discipline. I think those things went a long way towards helping me learn to value the contributions and efforts of others. Giving an employee respect and a chance to be heard goes a long way to having them buy-in to the environment you create in your dental practice.

This it the true application of all other skills learned that we will cover in other sections.

How you manage your relationships is very complex. Usually it is hard to manage in the group context, but rather you must train and have a relationship with each employee in a small setting like a dental office.

You need to have guidelines, expectations that are clearly laid out so there is no confusion, and you have to hold each employee accountable to those guidelines, both as an individual and as a group. It cannot be emphasized enough that you need to check in on each employee and see how they are doing because each person has a different set of wants and needs, and each one is motivated in a specific, personal way. Leading a team meeting and using a team message is good for some goals, but each goal and message needs to be personalized to fit the specific way each employee is best motivated.

The same approach needs to be used with patients also. The

old saying, "one size fits all," as far as treatment planning and acceptance go, is just that: old. Accept that a uniform approach to all patients will have limited success in the modern, digital world, with patients asking more questions and questioning our authority as a doctor more than some of the older generations. The older generation accepted authority more and would go along with what we suggested because we were the authority figure. I can't remember how many times I heard from my older patients, "Whatever you say, doc," or "You are the doctor." That is no longer the norm with younger patients, and we need to understand that we have to have a new approach, where we listen more, give more choices, and let the patient guide the fit and the readiness that they have in accepting treatment, with them in control of their choices.

5. MOTIVATION

In recent literature, the experts have added a fifth characteristic. That characteristic is Motivation, which drives people from within to achieve beyond expectations, both their own and everyone else's. They exhibit optimism in face of failure. Proving that they are motivated not necessarily by a big salary and a big title, but rather to achieve for the sake of achievement.

To identify this motivation in yourself and others, first is the passion for the work itself:

> Do you love dentistry, or just what it can bring you?
>
> Do you seek out creative challenges, love to learn, taking continuing education well beyond what is required?
>
> Do you take pride in a job well done?
>
> Do you look to learn the newest technology and new

approaches to your job?

Do you raise the bar when you accomplish a goal and keep score?

One of the last pieces is commitment to the group and to the profession. Do you stand up for your team and for your profession against the forces that are trying to take over our profession?

HOW EQ APPLIES TO DENTISTRY

EQ is at the core of leadership. Leadership is needed at all levels on the dental team, from the doctor to the officer manager, to the hygienists and each dental assistant in their respective areas. This applies to self-management in their tasks and how they interact with patients, as well as how they react to instruction and management by supervisors.

People on the team needs to know themselves well enough to be able to control their emotions in all the relationships that are inevitable in a team environment and a service industry.

1. EQ AFFECTS COMMUNICATION SKILLS

Everyone needs to be able to be able to listen to instructions and know how to react. Listening is an important skill when working in a service industry.

With Your Team
There are many levels of communications needed within the team. There are the doctor-team communications and the team-team communications.

The doctor needs to find a way to express their vision for the team and how the practice is to be run. There is the technical training needed and how to cooperate with each other. There is the division of work duties, and all the systems on how the practice is to work. There is the need to build trust between all team members, the ability to have conflict and how to work through it in a productive manner, which will lead the team to buy into the goals of the office.

With Your Patients

If you don't communicate with patients, you will have no business. You have to learn how to get them into your office, and how to treat them in a way they want to be treated so that they will want to stay. You need to learn how to educate your patients to understand their dental needs and for you to be able to understand their life circumstances so that you can figure out their readiness for dental work and how that all fits together when discussing the type, and expense, of the work recommended.

So often dentists were trained to know one, best way to do dentistry. That has changed over the years, and as a profession, we will have to learn to listen better to find what people want, when they want it, and will have to discuss price in a way most of us are not comfortable with. This includes the traditional intake, exam and consultation method we have been using forever.

2. EQ EFFECTS ADAPTABILITY/FLEXIBILITY

The new generations don't just blindly accept how we want to do it. Thanks to the advent and popularity of the internet, many patients will be able to research different options and get a "second opinion" on the world wide web.

Knowing yourself, how you react when challenged, and how to respond to keep yourself in harmony with others is the essence of EQ. More and more, we as professionals, will have to answer WHY from our patients, because they do not react in the same way our older patients traditionally have. We will have to adapt to the new communication style of the younger patients and we will have to be more flexible than we have been in the past.

3. EQ EFFECTS TREATMENT ACCEPTANCE

We will need to ask the right questions and really get to know the readiness and fit of what we are offering in these changing times. It is not enough to declare that someone has a need and expect them to accept everything. I use to wonder why people would say no, say nothing and not return, or say yes and call back to say no. There were things in their lives that were more important to them than healthy teeth. They were not ready to do optional, cosmetic procedures. They had illnesses. They had a kid's college tuition that was due next month. Their car had just broken down. When they were ready, if they trusted me and stayed in the practice, they did the treatment, slowly, on an as-needed basis.

4. EQ EFFECTS INTERVIEW SKILLS

You have to be emotionally intelligent enough to listen, and be able to interpret what the patients are saying. When they have life issues, you need to be able to understand and ask what is in the way of full treatment. You need to read body language that tells you something isn't clicking. You can also use body language to ask questions about their readiness for the treatment and whether the treatment and price fit into their life at this moment. If it doesn't, then explore which alternatives can keep them healthy, or perform the work in installments with treatment that fits into their situation.

5. EQ EFFECTS JOB SATISFACTION

If you cannot control your emotions, if everything stresses you out, if all your employees drive you crazy, if you don't like seeing certain patients or types of patients, you are not going to be happy or satisfied with your job. You need to learn to recognize what your stressors are and how to respond on an internal level in order to help control the emotions that make your job unsatisfactory. People with low EQ will remain poorly motivated and unhappy in their job. People who know themselves and what makes them stressed and how to control their emotions will be much happier.

6. EQ EFFECTS YOUR STRESS LEVEL

Your Personal Stress Level
If you are the team leader, your stress level will dictate the office stress level. Sometimes unconsciously, I may have let a problem in the office show on my face or in my tone when talking to the team or a patient. I had some long-time patients that said to me a couple times when I had come out of a room with a difficult patient and into their treatment room, "What's eatin' you Doc?" It will show in you voice, your face, your body language and sometimes, your attitude.

Try some breathing exercises between patients if you are having a bad day. The next patient didn't cause the stress of the last patient and deserves your best. If a patient picks up on this, most likely your chairside assistant notices your mood as well.

The Team Stress Level
As I said, your mood, your stress will rub off on the whole team. If you want to have a positive attitude and low stress in the office, the most effective thing you can do is improve your EQ, and your attitude to make everyone a lot happier.

Which Personality Traits Are Affected By EQ & How Do They Apply To Dentistry?

As a business leader and a dentist, you always have a choice when it comes to how you behave:

1. Pessimism OR Optimism

Do you think the day is going to go well? Do you think you are going to have a successful practice, gain new patients, save for retirement, buy the new equipment, get a new home, educate you children, and stay married? If you do, you are an optimist and much more likely to actually accomplish your goals than pessimists.

2. Encourager OR Critic

This applies to both patients and team members, but since you are with the team much more, we will focus on how these personality traits can affect your team members. You will find that encouraging the team as they learn new things and even when they fumble the ball, will enable them to be more likely to thrive under your leadership and they will always try to do better.

3. Self-Motivated OR Needs Direction From Others

Self-starters are more successful. If you are the boss, who is going to give you direction? If you can hire people who need little or no direction, your team will excel. The modern practice does not provide the doctor/producer with ample time to manage people who need a lot of guidance, so if you have team members who are needier in that department, you might consider hiring an office manager who can put more time and attention into their professional development.

4. Empathetic OR Self-Centered

Most doctors are somewhat self-centered and empathy often has to become a learned skill. Empathy is at the center of EQ, because you have to be able to put yourself in other people's shoes in order to understand the full scope of their reaction. For example, empathy can mean the difference between when a patient is ready to have fine dentistry and when they are hesitant because they are in a life situation where they have to wait or have compromised treatment.

5. Synergistic OR Afraid of Failure

Are you mature enough to recognize that others on your team have skills you do not possess or have less of? Are you mature enough to let them take control of some part of the team effort without you suffering some emotional trauma? At some point there is the need for trust, where you have to give up the fear of failure because you are not in control of everything, and let someone else with good skills do what you can't do. You have to have emotional intelligence and maturity to let this happen.

6. Transparent OR Closed

Disclosing parts of yourself, if ever so slightly to your patients, is one of the first trust-building acts dentists need to do in the initial patient interview. If you are aloof and arrogant, you will not build the trust that is needed for a long-term relationship with your patients.

7. Respectful OR Disrespectful

What doctor, in his or her right mind, would disrespect a new patient, or a patient of record, if they want to keep them as patients? In all honesty, you do not have the luxury of acting that way. The same goes with employees. You may disrespect a team member, but studies show that if that happens, productivity intentionally goes down by staff treated in that way. Don't fool yourself by telling yourself that you can act any way you like because you write the check, as that will always backfire on you.

8. Apologize When Wrong OR Can't Ever Be Wrong

I am sad to say, I get to practice the apology part of this more than I would like. It is important to both family relationships and team relationships to know when to say you are sorry. Obviously, you need to do the same for patients. Especially in this digital age, one mad patient can run off ten patients if you do not listen to grievances and repair fences by apologizing when you are in the wrong.

9. Self Aware ("Mindfulness") OR Clueless

Are you clueless? Are you drifting along, letting life happen to you? Or, are self-aware, knowing how your emotions are affected by certain situations, and what you should do as the proper response to the stimuli. This goes back to the first lesson of EQ: Knowing Yourself. The more you are aware, the better you lead.

10. Listener OR Lecturer

Most sales people make the mistake of talking 80% of the time, and listening 20% of the time. We are trained to be experts in our field. We want people to think we know what we are doing. The best salesmen listen more and talk less, so let us take that lesson from the good salesmen. People want to know what the benefits of your treatment will be for them, not how great you are.

11. Likeable OR Cold

All studies of sales show that people will buy from people they like. The transparency mentioned above is the first step to likeability. Even if it is just a little self-disclosure, it is a start to a friendship.

12. Pay Attention OR Thinking of Next Answer

When you are one-on-one with a team member or a patient, do you find yourself paying full attention to what they are saying, or are you thinking about the next thing YOU are going to say instead of being fully engaged in their tale? As a dentist, this can be quite common. We are thinking about what we are going to recommend, and how we can dominate the conversation instead of REALLY listening to what the patient is saying. In most cases we will miss a lot of the obvious detail and all of the subtle details. Learn to be a better listener.

13. Adjust To Team Personalities OR Treat Everyone The Same

Do you know your team member's individual personality traits, preferences and styles? The DiSC personality profile gives you several generalized clues into how people prefer to be treated and approached. There are four DiSC categories, each with preference on how they act and interact. In the general population, about

25% are each type. If you are a Dominant person and treat all your team like they are Dominant, you have a 75% chance you will be interacting in a less that optimum fashion. You need to approach people based on their own strength, not yours, if you want maximum harmony. It is a good exercise to learn how to work with people by studying this simple personality study.

14. Giver OR Taker
Most great leaders are Servant/Leaders, who look out for teammates and give more than they take. A greedy or self-centered approach rarely works for the long haul. Usually, a great leader will receive much better help from his team if he is giving into their career and life in an effort to make them better. Making others better will improve how your rate of return, especially if you have good people with you.

15. Non-Judgmental OR Judgmental
A leader has to judge actions on occasion, but leaders with good EQ will dig deep and use the empathy he has to discern the situation without judgement, until all facts are known. Then a judgement can be made with full information. In this situation I am referring to a recurring attitude of the leader. Does he automatically judge something with partial information or pre-judge because of a prejudice?

16. Demanding Accountability of Team OR No Control
These are two polar opposites. In some cases, a lack of EQ will not let the boss confront situations, and the team runs wild, with little control. On the other hand, if you have taken the right steps to expect accountability, it is not overreach to expect it. If you don't

set high standards, no one on the team will rise to the occasion.

17. Managing Conflict For Positive Results OR Ignore/Deflect Conflict

Unfortunately, it is near impossible to avoid conflict in a team-working environment. Will you ignore or deflect the conflict? Pretend it didn't happen? Put it off to another day, which is in fact, forgetting about it? To grow teamwork or a good personal relationship, we have to confront conflict head on, and manage it in a way it does not destroy relationships. Rather, it should help build open conversations and build a transparency on the team where you can confront real issues in a way people will experience growth. As I had mentioned earlier, Wiley Co., is developing an instrument that can help your group work through this process in a productive way that can be part of teamwork training.

18. Addressing Need OR Pitching

All sales transactions at some point have a "pitch." That is not necessarily a bad thing, it is just a part of the sales process. The emphasis here is that as a service provider and a servant leader, you need to find out what your client's need is, what they want, how your services fit into their life and whether they are ready and able to afford it. It is not bad to try to convince someone to buy from you. In fact, it is necessary if you are going to stay in business. Better long-term relationships will be born if you ask what the need is and work your pitch around need, desire, fit, and readiness of the buyer.

19. Build Trust OR Close Too Soon

I often wondered how the restorative gurus went from first

appointment to a $40,000 treatment two days later. I believe those type doctors have people coming to them already knowing they have complex needs, the doctor sorts that out immediately, and proceeds with the complex treatment. That is atypical in the world of most doctors, however, and people come in mostly not knowing that they need complex treatment, or they have simpler problems. If a patient is clueless of need, trust in you and belief that they actually have a problem are the first steps towards awareness and acceptance that they need work. Trust is established by listening and making the patient aware of the problem first, which often takes a long time. Many small steps are often required before they will accept anything we say.

20. Understanding AND Awareness

Understanding the life circumstance of the patient is essential in determining whether a course of treatment is the right fit for a patient. Are they living hand to mouth, or are they affluent? Do they have urgency to get something done, or not? What are their specific life events that cause that urgency? Is there a daughter getting married in a few months? Do they want something cosmetic done immediately, before a complex exam, so that they will look presentable for a social event in two weeks?

The right questions need to be asked so that you approach that correctly and in a timely manner.

Awareness is whether or not they know they have a dental issue. Periodontal problems are often undetected in people who do not get regular periodic care. Because of that, patients do not understand the effect of having missing teeth or letting a tooth decay for so long that they end up with an abscess. We are usually pretty good at educating people after the fact, but since so many people come in with only partial awareness, we have to learn how to manage their flawed expectations.

21. Advocate OR Self-Serving

The old traditional model of treatment planning and presentation was for the most part self-serving in its structure: Discover, Diagnose, Present to Close. If you were altruistic, at the core, you were presenting things that the patient probably needed, with the variations being what was optional. We were taught to present the ultimate, complete treatment, A to Z, all at once, right now.
The Advocate model will recognize optimum treatment, but then advocates for the patient, taking into consideration all the things we discussed earlier: Awareness, Fit, Readiness, and Life Events. That is really going to probably work out best for you in the end, because if you ignore those things, a lot of the time, people will not return and you don't get to treat them at all. By finding out more about their situation, you can be their advocate, and recognize it by asking whether they can do the complete treatment now, or need to do it a little at a time.

22. Our Expertise OR Accepting Patient Decisions

One of the hardest parts is accepting the patient's decision about how they proceed, or do not proceed, with treatment. We feel compelled to educate them into doing what we want. We know that they need our expertise and that they would be better off if they did it immediately. But only they can decide what they want or need to do based on what is best for them, not what we think is best. We need to step back and let them own their problem in their way, so that it fits into their life is best for them at the time. We have fulfilled our obligation to tell then what we think is best, but it is also our obligation to honor what they think they need. We can help them get to a stable, healthy condition that falls short of perfect, and leave it at that until they are ready for the full treatment.

23. Balanced Life OR Too Much of Something
Do you work all the time? Do you have a good family life? Do you work too little? Do you play golf to the detriment of your practice? I had an orthodontist tell me once, "If a dentist shoots more than 80, he has no business being on the golf course, and if a dentist shoots less than 80, he has no business." That is a great example of why it's best to choose all things in moderation. The Pankey philosophy stuck with me early in my career because it spoke of a Balance in Life and Practice. It helped me recognize when I was out of balance, even though it didn't necessarily help me learn how to balance anything better.

24. Know Your "Why " OR Concentrate On "What or How"
Simon Sinik's book, "Start with Why," gave me insights into why I work. I will not try to tell you what is the correct why for you because that is a journey you must take on your own. Why do you get up in the morning? What is your inspiration? What are your core beliefs that drive you each day?

I love working with people and I loved dentistry for the nearly 45 years that I was in practice. I also now love to teach in training programs, because I want to pass on the knowledge I have picked up over these many years. Even though it is hard for me to physically do the job of dentistry, my mind still works pretty well.

So many times we concentrate on the what and the how in dentistry, focusing on the clinical and technical parts. Those are a prerequisite to being a good dentist, but it isn't what will make you get up in the morning and love going to work.

25. Urgency Addiction OR Make the Main Thing the Main Thing

Do you work through lunch on emergencies? Do you do too few productive procedures because your day is full of short, unproductive things that "just have to get done today"? Do you always add that one extra patient who just can't wait until tomorrow?

If you are running a business, you need to reserve time to do the Main Thing first. I marked off emergency time every day, after I had prioritized the dentistry that would make my production for the day. If poor production is a problem, look at the structure of your appointment book first, to see if you are making 'the main thing the main thing."

26. Treatment Choice OR My Way Is the Only Way

This isn't a comparison. The old, traditional way to treatment plan and present was that you are the doctor so you know what is best for the patient. If you don't do it the way I suggest, then there is no other option but to go somewhere else. That is a "My way or the highway" scenario. So many times we were trained to think that the optimum treatment was one size fits all, the way to treatment plan everyone. Of course, that does not work well these days and we need to look into the desires of patients, within the bounds of good dentistry, done on their timetable.

Symptoms Of Low EQ

1. LACK OF EMPATHY

Empathy is not sympathy. Sympathy is focused on yourself and what is your reaction to some else's problem. Empathy is being able to place yourself in another person's situation and having appropriate feelings and actions based on how knowing their situation is affecting them. So much of today's world is self-centered. How does something affect ME? Is it my problem? Do I care whether they are having a problem?

We don't have to save the whole world, but if you have no empathy, people will probably be able to pick up on the fact that you are in this work just for what you can gain.

2. TEMPER

Temper is usually a sign of a lack of self-control. There are cases of righteous indignation and righteous anger in the face of cruelty and injustice. That is not in play here. I am talking about taking such a strong stance on an issue, that it is an inappropriate overreach of emotion, including an overreaction to something that is minor. My point here is that it would be an exaggerated reaction to something that could have been talked through and an agreement made without the extra emotion.

What could cause this? It could be something pre-existing in a person's history. It could be they were having a bad day, or it could be that there is some underlying emotional problem or situation the person is having that particular day. It is hard to deal with a person who is having this strong emotion and often this has to be defused before any resolution can happen.

3. SELF-CENTERED

The root cause of being self-centered is selfishness, greed, and pride. This person will have trouble in relationships and in leadership. Most often they will blame others for anything that upsets them. They are always trying to make the fast buck and take care of their interest first over others. I'm sure you can apply that to a dentist you know who puts their own well-being and monetary gain above what is best for their patients. Not everyone needs a full-mouth rehab, and sometimes that is motivated by greed and selfishly wanting to make more money for themselves.

4. POOR LISTENING SKILLS

There are 4 common symptoms of poor listening skills:

> a. Interrupting. Talking when others aren't through their sentence or thought. Talking is not listening and interrupting is very disrespectful. It will shut down any kind of interaction that may be going on.
>
> b. Not paying attention. Thinking of what you are going to say next while someone else is still talking is a sign that you think that what you want to say is more important than what the speaker is saying. You will stop concentrating on what they are saying, and in a lot of cases, they will be able to see that and react to your inattention.
>
> c. Ignoring their question. If you just continue with your thought or your monologue instead of focusing on their concerns is another sign of poor listening.
>
> d. Being distracted. Texting or reading messages while they

are talking shows an obvious disregard for what they are saying.

5. DOMINANT BEHAVIOR

Dominant personalities most often want to be in control. There are several ways that behavior can be manifested:

a. Ignoring others. They often consider their opinion to be supreme, so there is no reason to listen to another point of view. They often don't consider anything someone else has to say about an issue, and just go with whatever they consider important instead of listening to other opinions.

b. Overpowering others. If someone dares to express a contrary opinion, they often will abruptly and rudely push on by others either physically or verbally. With additional volume or speaking over others, they will make their point of view dominate the discussion.

c. Demeaning others. Name calling is often used and I have seen a dominant employer call his employees, dummies and stupid, ugly and lazy, to their faces. They are not in a position to lose their jobs, so they put up with this coarse and demeaning behavior.

d. Bullying others. This goes hand in hand with demeaning. A person in power can often get their way by bullying. This is most often not physical, but rather an emotional and verbal attack to try to make someone feel unworthy, or weak by overpowering them.

6. POOR ADAPTABILITY

Familiarity is good at times, until it causes paralysis. Sometimes people get so used to doing their routine things a certain way, they are very resistant to change. Some examples of poor adaptability include:

a. Not being able to change with circumstances. In this fast changing world, the only thing that is constant is change. If you are not willing to learn in this world, you will be left far behind within a very short period time.

b. Reacting poorly to adversity. Poor EQ does not allow you to adapt. In any social setting or work, there is going to be conflict and adversity. We must learn how to harness that conflict and create a useful conversation with our coworkers to get understanding and buy-in to the team goals.

c. To affected by emotions. If you become upset and emotional easily, you will be out of control of your emotions. As you learn how you feel in certain situations, you can learn to raise your EQ.

d. Panic when plans change. The most extreme reaction to change is panic. In most cases, that is an overreaction that will not allow you to think straight or function well. It is an irrational reaction to something that is natural in nature because of the complexity of life which makes situations change from minute to minute.

How Low Dental EQ Affects Your Practice

Job Satisfaction

If the team has to work with someone who is not skilled in their EQ there can be several negative things that can happen:

1. Team Turnover
This will result when there is chronic discontent by employees. It can also be the result of a boss who blows up and reacts by firing people with little regard to their ability. Often turnover will be caused by poor emotional response to a situation that escalated without good cause. More often it is the slow drip of disrespect or lack of consistent supervision or guidance. People want to know what is expected of them, so they can have a sense of measurement in the job. A boss who does not set clear expectations, and then judges performance by an arbitrary measure will cause great damage to morale and eventually to employees leaving the team.

2. Subversion of team and productivity
People will intentionally underperform if unhappy and sometimes sabotage the workplace to show their displeasure in a passive aggressive way.

3. Incivility
A recent poll of 800 managers showed that there are significant costs to incivility including the intentional reduction in their work

effort, missing work, decreased quality of work, and lost time by other employees avoiding offenders. Most often, they will often take their frustration out on customers and many leave their jobs.

4. Poor Hiring Choices

If you are a leader with low EQ, you may make some bad hiring choices, much to the detriment of your practice.

I experienced poor results in hiring a trained dental assistant at one time in my practice. I decided to try a different way of finding employees that blended with our team. I asked one of my hygienists if she knew anyone who was energetic, friendly and would have an appreciation of a job that had benefits and would get to work with a wonderful group of motivated people. She immediately told me of a young lady who worked at a convenience store a couple miles from our office. I had my hygienist call her and ask if she would like to interview for the job. I decided to do an off-site interview, in secret, before the formal interview. I went to the store, and walked around, looking at potato chips. She was at the counter, smiled when we made eye contact and asked if she could help me with anything. I told her I was looking for a certain type chips. She came from behind the counter and started showing me different chips, and told me of the qualities of a couple of them. I spoke with her a little more and thanked her for her help. She rang up my purchase and I left. She showed me several things in those couple minutes. She smiled, she engaged me as a customer, she answered my questions, she offered her opinion about the goods, she came from behind her barrier to engage me. She could operate the machine to check me out. She was the type person I wanted to hire.

When she came in to the formal interview the next day, you can imagine the look on her face. She didn't quite know what to say. I told her I had already interviewed her, she had passed with flying colors and I could train her to do the dental stuff, and she already possessed the most important qualities I was looking for in a new employee. All that was left to do was to negotiate salary, benefits, and when she could start. When I retired, she had been with me over ten years and she still works for the doctor that bought my practice. The lesson here: hire for attitude, train for skills.

5. Rude Employees
Employees often are rude in front of customers, which causes loss of customers. I have witnesses inappropriate behavior at retail stores, in which one clerk would be talking to another about how they are mad at someone else on staff, or how their spouse had acted poorly the night before. In those cases, they have not been taught that their job is a service job, and they represent their company. Their job is to make me feel good about spending my money in that store, and that my experience depends primarily on how they interact with me, since the picking out of the items I buy is pretty much a transactional thing in which I have little emotional investment.

The same interactions happen in a dental office. Most clients have made their mind up about whether they are going to like your office by the time they have talked to your receptionist and checked in at the front office. The first five minutes can often determine whether they will return for a second visit.

6. Poor Team Satisfaction
This sometimes shows up as thoughtlessness instead of actual malice. Team members may just go through the motions, with very

little concern for quality or service if they are unhappy. Patients can pick up on everyone's mood in a dental office, from front to back, from assistant to doctor. Poor attitudes will subvert any good attempt to have a positive influence. Keep the team happy so that the patients will sense that and return.

7. Poor Communication
Low EQ will result in team members not having the capacity to read other team members emotions and not be able to give the appropriate response to questions or orders. They may misunderstand others and get into verbal fights because of poor understanding. They will not know how to respond to a patient's needs and interfere with good teamwork.

8. Less Cooperation
If a team member does not understand a situation, they may not have the capacity to be a help in a situation where there needs to be teamwork to complete a task. They may take exception to a leadership style and intentionally not cooperate.

9. Production
If the team is not working well together, it is like having a cog out of a machine, throwing off the efficiency of the whole machine. If everyone is not doing their assigned part, the team works less efficiently, making production poor.

10. Insufficient Collections
Collections are a function of communication of what is expected, and asking with confidence and politely that you expect payment. Whoever is doing collections need to be emotionally intelligent

enough to understand the clients, and be able to use several techniques to convey our expectations. If someone cannot read some else's emotional state, they will probably not handle collections well.

11. Fewer Referrals

This is also a communications skill, as you have to do two things well to get referrals: the first is to treat people well, giving them great service and the second is to be able to ask and actually let them know that you want and need more referrals. That is a developed skill that has to come from the leader, and practice until it is done well.

12. Loss of Patients

Poor service causes patient loss. If there is an attitude problem, it is a natural thing to lose patients.

13. Poor Team Training

Both leaders and team members can be responsible for team training and if either has low EQ, there will either be no training or poor training. If a team member does not have the capacity to understand the training, it is a waste of time to try and if the leader sees no need to spend the necessary time to train, there will not be growth.

14. Cycle of Stress

In interactions that are stressful, there is a cycle that makes it get worse and worse.

As a person is stressed, they will withdraw from contact to try to reduce or remove the stress. The withdrawal will create a situation where the person will not totally understand what is going on around them, which can lead to the people they are interacting with having a bad impression of them, when actually the behavior wasn't because they were behaving badly, they were just trying to avoid the stress. When they make a bad impression, the respondent will send verbal or physical cues to the person that they are not happy with their response, which causes more stress. From there, with the increased stress, they will have an even more exaggerated contracted behavior as the cycle continues, escalating more and more.

HOW TO IMPROVE YOUR EMOTIONAL INTELLIGENCE

1. KNOW YOURSELF

Know your values and principles. Practice observing how you feel. After a while you will trust your emotions and get better at managing them. Set apart some time to reflect on how you feel. Pay attention to physical sensations and how you feel when you have different emotions. Pay attention to how you behave when you have different emotions.

You can only change behavior if you are aware of your actions and reactions. Read any physical cues, like tension, tightening muscles, clenching jaws and posture. Do you move closer to confront or do you relax?

I know what I just wrote is counter-intuitive for a dentist. When do you have time for quiet time? How do you balance this with a busy practice and family life? I said this is simple, but not easy. Although, what is the alternative? If you do not grow your EQ, just like your clinical skills, how are you going to become a mature individual, mastering your emotions as well as you do your restorative ability?

2. MANAGE EMOTIONS

Take responsibility for your feelings and behaviors. If you lash out, that is on you. Practice responding rather than reacting. Reacting is an unconscious, base brain, limbic reaction that is not processed in your frontal cortex. There is not reason there, just reaction.

Practice empathy with self and others. Ask yourself "why am I feeling this way?" and "why am I doing this?" If you practice, and listen to yourself, you will get answers. Create a positive environment to be able to have better EQ. Think about what going well and the reasons why you are grateful. You can figure out what has a negative impact to your emotions and what is positive, and try to stay out of situations that drag you down. Instead, increase the number of positive events in your life.

This is a lifetime process you have to work at in order to improve, even if it is little by little.

Notice how emotions and behaviors are connected. These are some of the coupled emotions that often trigger specific behaviors:

- Embarrassment may trigger withdrawal.
- Anger may trigger a raised voice.
- Overwhelmed may trigger pain and loss of concentration.

Here are some ways you can learn to manage difficult emotions:

A. Avoid judging your own emotions. Emotions happen, so be kind to yourself. If you judge yourself, the condemnation you may feel could stop your progress because of guilt. Acknowledge the emotion, decide if it is a constructive or destructive emotion, and work on ways to have less of the destructive emotions. When you have a negative emotion, connect it to the reaction you are having.

Fully experience the positive emotions you have, including joy, and the satisfaction from the experience that is going on at the time. Learn how to feel these positive emotions more often. Tell yourself how you want to act and react, and move toward that emotion.

B. Recognize and control patterns. Once you recognize your emotions, you can then move to learn how to control these patterns. You may want to journal about your feelings, along with the events that triggered them and the reactions you had. Doing this over time will train your brain to recognize the patterns of emotion and reactions.

Decide how you are going to act, react and respond to each situation. There is a an old saying, "I am not going to die on that hill," which I have applied many times in my family relationships. Certain events cause conflict, and there have been many times when I have to decide if I am going to expend my emotional treasure to win a fight, or am I going to just let it go because the situation is not important enough to damage a relationship over something trivial.

C. Become more open-minded and agreeable. You can learn to do this through being understanding and using internal reflection on whether your response will be positive or negative. I don't mean being open-minded in the sense that you accept any and all points of view as equal. We all have a moral and ethical code that will need to be a gauge as to what we accept. On the other hand, we at least need to listen and understand other people's points of view and avoid being judgmental in non-critical issues. Whether we agree or not, we need to learn to listen and empathize with other's points of view, if not only for the sole purpose of keeping ourselves in balance.

D. Become more socially aware. We are in a diverse society and we need to do things like listen to debates without a predetermined prejudice. Consider both sides, look at subtleties in both arguments, and reflect on a differing argument's point of view.

3. KNOW OTHERS

A. Improve your Empathy Skills. Try to understand the feeling the other person is having in the situation. People have the same range of emotions and reactions that you do, but not in the same way for each and every situation. Just because you feel a certain emotion in a certain environment or situation, does not mean that you can assume someone is reacting exactly how you do. You must learn to put yourself in the other person's shoes.

When you see a person having a strong emotion, ask yourself, "How would I react to that?"

B. Learn active Listening. I attended a marriage relationship class with my wife, years ago that was about Active Listening and the skills were the same then as the ones you need to use today.

You can repeat what someone says to be sure you understand what they are saying to you to clarify the message. You can say something to the effect of, "Did I understand you said…..?" You can use "feel" words when discussing a situation. If you attack, people will fight back, but if you say, "I feel…" then it is hard for someone to argue about how you feel.

The key is to clarify what they said and what they meant by what they said. Do not jump to conclusions, let them be clear about their position. You can also take time to center your emotions by first getting them to clarify how they think and feel.

C. Learn to read body language. Are they open or closed, do they have their arms crossed or not? Are they clenching their fists? Are they making an angry face or smiling? Do they move closer and are they invading your private space? Are they apathetic or interested? Are they making eye contact or everting your gaze? Are they distracted and looking at social media instead of paying attention?

All these factors effect your communication with others, and the better you can read them, the better you can judge how you are communicating with others.

4. MANAGE YOUR RELATIONSHIPS

Understand the effect you have on others. Do you make people nervous, cheerful or angry? What happens to the conversation when you come in the room? Does your tone of voice or delivery have an effect on others?

If you have negative influences you need to ask yourself, is this what I want? If not, look at the patterns and actions you need to change. Ask others who are not intimidated by you to give you an honest assessment of how you affect others and make necessary changes.

Practice being emotionally honest. Do not put on "airs" in a way people can't tell how you feel. It is good to control your emotions in a predictable way, but you should also be transparent enough that people can tell when you are happy, angry or stressed. Be yourself so that others can 'read" you and have honest relations with you. That is not a license to be abusive or hurt others in the name of being yourself, since that is not an Emotionally Intelligent reaction.

5. TESTING, READING, TRAINING

There are standardized tests to give you a baseline EQ, but since this is skill that can be improved by study and self-improvement, I have personally seen very little use in the tests. There is a simple, free self-test I have taken that can be found online at www.emotionalintelligence.net, and other online sites. I took the assessment to inform myself, but I see very little application to general use.

There are many great books written on the subject, and there are institutes and colleges where you can be trained in Psychological testing and EQ, but I find the best way to practically use and improve your EQ is to read the books, study the principles, and spend enough time on self reflection and a few exercises—and practice, practice, practice—on knowing your own emotions and what causes them.

6. PRACTICING SKILLS AND WHAT YOU CAN CONTROL

We all have Emotional, Cognitive and Behavioral skills. Practicing these skills will lead to improvement.

A. EMOTIONAL SKILLS

1. Identifying and labeling feelings. This starts with self-awareness, observing yourself and recognizing and knowing the relationship between thoughts, feelings, and reactions.

2. Managing feelings. Monitoring "self-talk" to catch negative messages such as internal put-downs and realizing the basis of of the feeling.

3. Assessing the intensity of feelings. Having Insight, which is identifying patterns in your emotional life and reactions, and recognizing similar patterns in others.

4. Empathy. Understanding other's feelings and concerns and taking their perspective into account while appreciating the differences between people.

5. Managing feelings and communicating. Talking about feelings effectively, becoming a good listener and asking good questions, distinguishing between what someone does and my own reaction or judgement about it. Learning to actively listen by sending "I feel" messages instead of "you are" messages of blame.

6. Assertiveness. Being able to state you concerns without anger or passivity.

7. Self-Disclosure. Valuing openness and building trust in a relationship, being able to risk talking about your own

private feelings.

8. Self-Acceptance. Feeling pride and seeing yourself in a positive light, recognizing your strengths and weaknesses and being able to laugh at yourself.

9. Delaying gratification. Controlling impulses, which is your personal decision-making, examining your actions and knowing their consequences and knowing if these thoughts are ruling a decision. Taking personal responsibility for your life and accept consequences of your decisions and actions, accepting your feelings and moods.

10. Reducing stress. Learn the value of exercise and relaxation to calm you down.

11. Conflict resolution. Learn how to fight fair with others and work on a win/win model for negotiating compromise.

12. Knowing the difference between feelings and actions.

B. COGNITIVE SKILLS

1. Self-talk. Having an inner dialogue to cope with a topic or challenge or reinforce your behavior. This also includes having self talk about recognizing your emotions so that you can start the process of self-discovery.

2. Reading and interpreting social cues. For instance, how do social influences affect your behavior?

3. Planning and using strategies to problem-solve. This includes setting goals, identifying alternative actions and understanding consequences of actions.

4. Understanding behavior norms in yourself and others and society. Realizing what is your normal and also what is normal of those you interact with will lead to better understand and control.

5. Have a positive mental attitude. If you live in a negative world, you will not be able to make any change in your life. You will not see the hope in learning and your ability to have positive change.

6. Developing realistic expectations for yourself. I am not going to ever be a professional golfer, or even a scratch golfer (I am old, and I have had back surgery that will not allow me to take a full golf swing). I understand that, and have set my expectations a lot lower. This is emotionally intelligent. This is realistic. We need to be optimistic, but not unrealistic.

C. BEHAVIORAL SKILLS

1. Nonverbal skills. Using eye contact, facial expressions, tone, body language and gestures to show how you feel are all nonverbal methods of expressing yourself. Many studies show that non-verbal signals that we give off and receive have a big impact on impressions, even more than our verbal skills.

When we lean forward we show interest. When we look down without eye contact we will not build trust. If we smile we build rapport. We can say the same words with different tone and inflection, and get two totally different responses. These are all very important and bare studying to improve how we affect others.

2. Verbal cues. Making clear requests, responding effectively, resisting negative influences, using active listening, helping others and being a positive influence are all verbal ways of communicating effectively.

We need to specifically ask for what we desire, we need to get clarity from others about their requests. Actively listening, repeating what someone says to get clarity and showing empathy when someone has a problem are all big trust builders, so these skills need to be mastered.

SELF-AWARENESS EXERCISE

One of my favorite exercises to learn self-awareness is the 5-day log. Taking one hour in the day, and breaking it into ten-minute segments. Every ten minutes, make a note of the emotion you are feeling and the circumstances that created that emotion. Do this for only one hour each day, picking a different hour so that you will get a sample of the different circumstances that may happen at different times of the day.

Do this for five consecutive days, so that you will have thirty emotions caused by thirty circumstances. Then sit down and analyze. Take a marker and note similar emotions with one color. Mark each emotion with a different color. Look for similar circumstance and code them. Look for patterns of what creates certain emotions.

This is a time to be reflective and study what causes you to have certain emotions and to also look at how you reacted to these emotions. Can you make changes to negative stimuli or why you had these emotions? This is where you start to learn and start to create change.

7. FACTORS YOU CAN CONTROL

A. Attitude

Attitude is an internally controlled emotion. No one else makes you have a certain attitude. You have the control to have a good or a bad attitude. Circumstance in life may seem to cause someone to have a certain attitude, but the truth is, that attitude is a choice you make, even in the face of a bad situation.

B. Effort

You alone decides how hard you will work and how concentrated you are going to be when faced with a task or your life's work. Your physical well-being may effect you to some degree, especially if you have actual physical disabilities, but even with that, I am not talking about amount of performance, but rather the effort you put forth. You absolutely decide on how hard you will try in any situation.

C Direction

Most situations in life come to a point where you will make a right or left turn, you go forward or you go back. That is a cognitive decision also. You control most of these decisions.

D. Training

We all decided to go to professional school. We also will have to decide what continuing education we will take as we go through our professional life. That will create the next opportunities in our career. Deciding to become more emotionally intelligent is also a training choice. Either we will or we will not. We all have a finite number of hours and days we can study new skills. We can control which we will allow to take up our time.

E. Emphasis

I decided to learn cosmetic and restorative procedures and concentrate my learning and my practice in that area. More people are learning how to place and restore implants and to do sedation. That is their chosen emphasis. We all get to choose in this great profession, what path we want to follow.

F. Reaction

Most of what happens in a dental office every day involves various people coming in with their own set of life circumstances and their own reactions to what is happening in their life. How they interact with us will determine how we interact with them—we have to decide how we are going to act, or react. Having high EQ will help us to consider a lot of things before we respond, and hopefully we will act in a compassionate and empathetic way. We get to choose how we will react to everyone and every situation we meet, several times each day.

G. Skill

You get to make a conscious decision how skilled you will become. You can choose to continue your education, find mentors, and practice new skills so that you pass from novice to expert over a period of time. You get to choose how skilled you are and decide which skills you want to expand.

H. Leadership Style

We start in life with a specific IQ and with certain leadership skills that are somewhat environmental and second nature, but most leadership skills are learned in life. Through mentors, examples, parenting style, and through study and practice, trial and error, you can train yourself to become a better leader through sheer effort and determination. Certain mental shortcomings may be hard to overcome, but you can decide to be better, train and study and at the very least become much better than you would be naturally, without extra conscious effort.

I. Patient Approach

My DiSC personality style is a natural, strong "D", which stands for Dominance. My natural tendency is to want action—few words, just do it—and without too many niceties. Can you see where I may have needed some work?

We all have a prevailing personality style. Some people want to be friends, some want no conflict and some want things to be done precisely a certain way. Empathy was something that had to be a learned trait in me. I worked on it, I learned to listen better, and I adapted to what tendency the patient had, not the way I wanted to get things done. Everyone has a certain style. Everyone has to figure out the style of the person sitting in front of them is, and try to approach them in the patient's style, not their own. You can learn to recognize how people want to be approached.

You can change the way you act. It may not be easy, but if you want to succeed in life, you will learn to do this skill.

There is a quick and dirty way to get a feel for the person who is talking to you. It is an exercise from DiSC training, called "People Reading." Consider if this person is more fast-paced and outspoken or if they are more cautious and reflective. Draw a cross and place them either in the top or bottom. Then consider whether they are more questioning and skeptical, or if they are more accepting and warm. Place them in a left or right sides, accordingly.

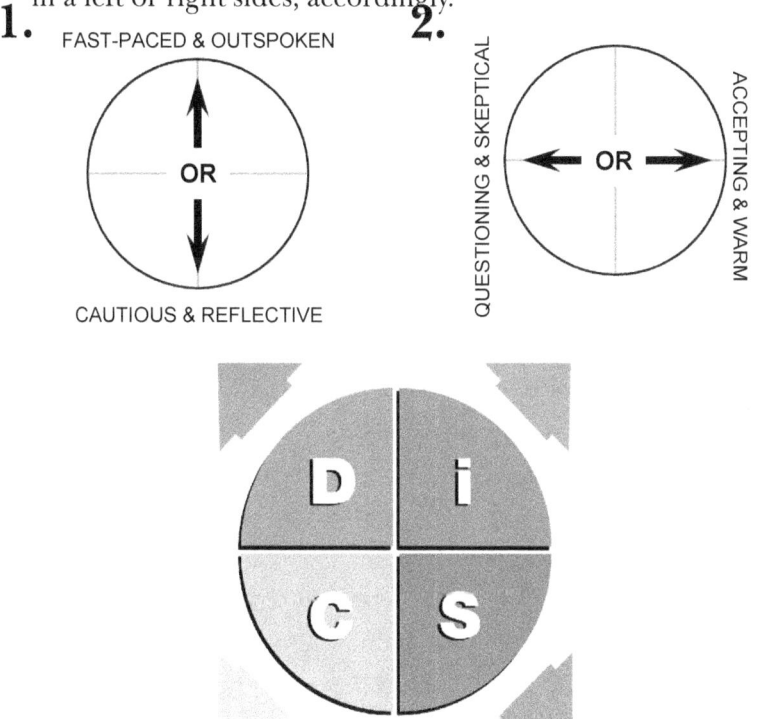

This makes four quadrants that make up the D-I-S-C style chart. Now combine this person's tendencies to determine this person's DiSC style. If they are fast-paced and questioning, they are a "D", which is a Dominant personality. If they are cautious and warm, they are a "S", and so on. Further DiSC study will teach you how to approach each of these for generalized styles. We are all a mix of all the styles, we just have one or two that we favor.

J. Staff Training

You can train your team or not. You can improve your team performance or ignore it. It is your choice. It takes constant monitoring behavior and many hours of individual attention, along with training sessions for the whole team.

8. BEHAVIORS PEOPLE WITH HIGH EQ DO NOT EXHIBIT

A. They do not get caught up in other people's drama. It is okay to empathize with others, but people with a high EQ don't let others dominate their well-being. Listen, give honest-but-loving advice when it applies, offer assistance when it does not interfere with your life, and don't be pulled into someone else's problem on such a personal level. People want others to side with them on issues that only affect them, so that they feel validated, but do not fall into that trap too.

B. They don't complain. Whining and grumbling are negative traits. People often act like a victim, but if you have a high EQ you don't blame others, but rather look for a constructive solution to the problem.

C. They don't always say yes. They will use self-control to keep from overcommitting and harming themselves with too much of a good thing at times and self-destructive behaviors. They are guided by self-control and their conviction about their core beliefs to limit doing everything that seem reasonable at the time. They will exercise their right to say no.

D. They don't gossip. Engaging in gossip is a behavior that aims to make you look better by cutting someone else down, and people with a high EQ are mature enough to avoid that behavior.

E. They don't count on others for their happiness or confidence. They are generally self-sufficient and have a contentment and peace of mind that comes from within or from a Higher Power that they believe in. Happiness and confidence are things that often cycle up and down, depending on circumstances in life. People with high EQ will not have such steep ups and downs because of their inner strength.

F. They don't have negative self-talk. They can tune out or silence the negative inner voices that can drag them down. That does not mean you have to chant some positive thinking mantra all day, but as a rule, they will have more positive self-talk than negative and it will show in all they say and do. It is a mind-set and an attitude that carries over to all parts of their life.

G. They don't dwell on the past. Remembering history is good in life, politics and business. If you don't remember the past, you will often repeat the same mistakes over and over. But remembering and dwelling on the past are two totally different things. If someone is looking back, they often remember why they can't do something because of a previous failure. Looking ahead will set you up to accomplish more and better things.

DENTAL BEHAVIOR THAT IS OUTDATED AND DOES NOT EXPRESS HIGH EQ

The Traditional Intake/Exam/Consultation Method

This old, traditional consultation method is an example of acting with a lack of Emotional Intelligence. This puts the doctor in the position of expert, and the patient as a passive recipient, prescribing what the patient needs and should do, with very little regard to what the patient says.

The outline of how this old method works:

   A. IDENTIFYING THE DISEASE
   We take x-rays, chart the disease, decay, missing teeth and all the pathology that is in the mouth. We mark it down, take photos and show it to them, often in a way they are embarrassed and do not enjoy. We probe the tissue, make them bleed, and stress that they have an infection in their mouth. We then figure out how much work they need done and quantify that for them.

   B. DESCRIBE THE TREATMENT PROCESS
   We then will talk about how many fillings they will need, how many teeth they will have to be removed, and whether or not they need surgery, and pain they will endure for how many visits and months. We discuss how they will look until the work is finished and how much the expense is going to be.

C. RAISING THEIR DENTAL IQ

We then tell them how badly they have been taking care of themselves, and we rattle on about brushing and flossing, and give them pamphlets and show them videos about the wonderful things we are going to do for them. This is usually done right after we have flooded their senses with their problems and we have introduced the cost, which usually shuts down listening from that point forward. They usually learn very little at this point in the process.

D. SELLING TECHNIQUES

Instead of talking about the benefits of the dental work we are going to do, we talk about how many years we have been doing this procedure and how we have bought at great expense all the new dental toys that aid us in allowing them to enjoy our great skill. The truth is that, beyond an elementary level, they don't care about you, because they are concentrating on themselves and all their fears, needs, demands on their time and money, instead of how great you and your toys are.

E. VISUAL AIDS

We have pictures of other patients that are Hollywood models with perfect teeth, or we pull out the skulls with implants drilled into the bone, so that they will feel great about you drilling into their jaw bone.

QUESTION: Does this make the patient FEEL better? Are we selling ourselves, or are we discussing the benefits the patient will get from pursuing treatment?

Past a very superficial level, does a patient really care if you have had 1000 hours of post-grad study in whatever you are selling? Once the trust is established and they feel comfortable you are competent, the rest is not necessary.

If we truly exercise EQ in our exams, we will not try to impress others, but rather focus on the patient's needs by asking probing questions, showing an empathy for their current situation, and find the appropriate treatment for them at this specific time in their life. That means understanding others and managing relationships, which are two of the five skills of EQ.

A different way of conducting a new patient exam starts with the phone interview by the receptionist. She will ask questions that explore exactly what the new patient wants to happen on this first visit. We need to find out if they have something that is really pressing. What is their primary focus? By addressing that initially, you are saying yes to their primary needs, which builds trust.

When they come in, you should interview the patient, building on the initial discussion to let them know you are listening to them. The rest of the appointment will discover basic needs and address the primary concern, either by doing something simple, or quickly reappointing to do that service.

Once this is done, you as a practitioner can move on to more complex problems. It is important for you to listen to them, before they can hear you.

Exercises You Can Use To Improve Your Emotional Intelligence

1. STUDIES AND BOOKS

The study of Emotional Intelligence started in earnest when Daniel Goleman started his brain research in the late 1980's and early 1990's. He published his book, "Emotional Intelligence," in 1995. He worked with Richard Boyatzis and Annie McKee to write several other books on the topic. It has since ballooned into a whole new division of psychology. For a quick scan of various works, I suggest Harvard Business School's "10 Must Reads On Emotional Intelligence," which features ten articles that cover a wide range of EQ topics.

2. MEASUREMENT AND TESTING

Some large specialty companies have EQ testing, but I feel that you can use a subjective approach for most tasks and jobs, instead of paying a large sum of money. Once again, Daniel Goleman offers a variety of free resources on his website, including assessments to help measure emotional intelligence.

3. SELF STUDY AND REFLECTION

A good starting point may be a Wiley, DiSC personality profile to find what your communication style is and build up from there. That profile will identify several traits a person has and the differences between the four general types. The report also tells you how to best get along with others and how you like to be approached. Almost all people need improvement in EQ, so everyone can benefit from completing a profile.

Wiley has an instrument based on the DiSC instrument in development called Productive Conflict, which will identify your behavior and tendencies when you are in conflict. How we react and handle our relationships with others is a big element in EQ. Spending quiet time and meditation, reflecting on your emotions, deciding what is important, reading and reflecting on how the information pertains to you, your life, your goals, and where you are in the process of personal development, are all ways to improve yourself.

4. PRACTICE THE NEW SKILL

You did not learn to cut a two surface preparation in a bicuspid in one day. You did not learn to drive a car or learn to swim in one day. All new skills, either mental or physical, take relentless practice to master. It is the same with improving your Emotional Intelligence. The skills are simple, but learning them is not easy.

For me, the hardest part is the discipline to examine my emotions over and over again. There are times I am in a situation that I do not want to be reflective and empathetic and thoughtful. There are times when I am so tired I don't feel like being reflective, I simply want to react. It is like any new habit, you have to repeat it until it become a part of the way you think and act. Simple, but definitely not easy.

5. DON'T GIVE UP

When I first discovered Emotional Intelligence, I was also studying DiSC personality profiles and how different people with different styles could take a simple questionnaire and get a good feel about their general tendencies.

I discovered that in my city, there was a clinical psychologist who had done some study in this field and had written about EQ's impact on how they approached their life and other people. Since I couldn't readily find any simple measurement tools to use like I could DiSC, I reached out to this expert.

I had met him years earlier in another type environment and I knew his credentials and his reputation. I was ready to be enlightened by this master. We met for lunch and had some polite talk before I asked him the big question I had: if there was any way I could find some instrument to use to measure and interpret someone's EQ.

He bluntly and flatly told me that I did not have the training and capacity to be able to administer and interpret such an instrument.

Since then, I have learned that there are schools and institutes run by psychologists that train you to do this. I wasn't interested in spending thousands of dollars to attend one of these schools at this point in my career, but I do understand that there are places that you can buy instruments and have the people on their staff interpret the findings and give you feedback of what a person's current status is with their EQ.

I now feel that a numerical EQ status may have limited value to most dentists. You are not going to be testing incoming patients and I think a subjective evaluation of your team members, using something like DiSC will give you enough insight about most people for a preliminary assessment.

Unless you are hiring a CEO or President of a large company, it is more important to work on listening skills as a way of improving your EQ, and to self develop your own team, using the insights in this book.

Wiley Company, who owns DiSC assessment instruments, is now working on a beta test of an extension of the DiSC line of products to include in instrument that help with Productive Conflict, part of Pat Lencioni's, "Five Dysfunctions of a Team." This instrument could be a key added evaluation to help with both teamwork and EQ, by evaluating how you think and react when in conflict, observing your own primal, first thoughts that may not be productive, and how to develop alternative thoughts and actions. Does that sound like emotional intelligence? I think so.

Does Emotional Intelligence Improve With Age?

Well, yes and no.

YES

Being alive a long time and experiencing a lot in life, may accidentally increase your EQ. But if there is not intentional growth, the accidental growth will be minor. I believe that experience is a great teacher, and you will learn to handle situations better by trial and error. The more years you live, the more times you get to repeat a behavior or a situation, and you will get better. I still believe that the intentional learning will be far greater than the accidental or incidental.

NO

Other than the incidental increase, there are several reasons that EQ will not be raised significantly unless there is intent, including:

- A. BEING DUMB. I know that this is an insensitive and unpopular word, but some people do not have the brain capacity to learn complex or introspective skills. Life just sort of happens to them and they are reactive instead of engaged. This is different from the second reason, which is listed below.

- B. IGNORANCE. Being unaware of how they can change, what they can change, or the refusal to look at change, is, for the most part, not a capacity situation, but a decision driven by a lack of information or poor information.

C. BLIND SPOT. They do not see that they need to improve. This can be across the full spectrum of EQ or just in certain areas. If you are not aware, you cannot change.

D. HARD WORK. Learning a new skill is hard work. Setting reminders to do the mental exercises and dissecting how you feel with the different circumstances takes an intentional effort. Like any discipline, you have to think about it, remind yourself to do it and then spend the time to work on it, over and over. It is not a one time learning experience.

E. UNWILLING TO MAKE CONSCIOUS DECISION TO CHANGE. Many people are fine just like they are and do not want to change anything. After all, ignorance can be bliss, so there is no immediate need to change. The perceived gain has to be more than the pain you have to go through to accomplish the desired change. Some people do not want any pain at any price, so they avoid what is needed to change their behavior.

F. TIME. As referenced under work, time is an element of the effort for change. This is a long-term or even a lifetime commitment to the learning and to the change. If you have too much on your plate already, and you haven't sorted out what is important, there may not be time to add another thing to your growing to-do list. Others don't see the importance, and just don't want to dedicate time to this change.

Benefits To Raising Your EQ

1. PERSONAL BENEFITS

   a. DECIDING WHICH BATTLES TO FIGHT
   When you understand your own emotions, and become mindful of what you feel when a conflict arises, you can better make decisions about what you are willing to stand up for, and actually fight for your cause. One of the greatest advantages of learning about your emotions and learning to control how you will act and react is that you understand that you are not going to waste emotional energy to have an argument about something that is trivial.

   b. STRESS
   You will have less stress if you learn how to manage your emotions rather than allow them to be a crazy rollercoaster in your brain, going up and down when stressors come into your life.

   c. BETTER MENTAL HEALTH
   Recognizing stress coming from different situations gives you the first step toward reducing your stress. If you know getting into certain situations is going to cause stress, you can take mental and physical actions to either avoid those situations or learn better coping mechanisms to reduce stress. Reducing stress has a direct effect to improve your mental health.

d. BETTER HEALTH

Less stress equals better health. Our emotional health will have a direct effect on our physical health. Better mental health equals better physical health. Added stress has been proven to lead to weight gain, high blood pressure, and cardiovascular issues

e. BETTER FAMILY RELATIONSHIPS

Any tool you can use to help you understand others is a tool that will help you get along with everyone better, including your family. Since you are usually with family more than anyone else in your life, it naturally will spill over into better family relationships. In families, there are often more situations that can create tension, since emotions and charged situations happen in family life.

f. LESS BLAMING, MORE ACCEPTANCE

Empathy is one of the EQ skills that will result in seeing the other person's point of view, and try to understand their argument better. Empathy can help you avoid placing blame or attacking another person without processing how you handle conflict and trying to look for alternatives before blaming.

g. PRIORTIZING LIFE'S CHOICES

So many times, people are not active participants in their life choices. So many people play the victim, abdicating their responsibility regarding how their life turns out. With high EQ, you will be the boss of your life. By taking responsibility of the things you can control instead of just riding what will probably be a less enjoyable life, you can take responsibility and control of the bulk of the things in your life. On top of that, if you prioritize what is most important, and what you will do first, or not at all, your life will be much more fulfilling.

h. PRIORITIZE BETTER

So often, people do things that are urgent, rather than what is important. The noise you get from a person who demands you do something for them right now often overwhelms the really important things that we really need to do to make our lives more profitable and enjoyable.

We need to have the strength of character to resist the urgent. The way I scheduled my time in the later years of my practice, was to make sure I did my profitable procedures and my enjoyable procedures early in the day. That allowed me the time to do the less profitable things AFTER the important part of making the office profitable was complete. This gave me peace about doing whatever came in the afternoon because our day was already successful by lunch.

This should extend to other things is life, like family time, and spiritual and emotional refreshment. There should be a time for those so that you can fill up your emotional gas tank each day.

2. BUSINESS BENEFITS

a. OVERLAP WITH PERSONAL BENEFITS

You can carry over all personal benefits to your business.

Most dentists work for themselves, so you are the business and your own personal emotional intelligence will be the main factor of success or failure in your business. If you work for someone else, your ability to get along with your boss will also effect your future as well.

b. BETTER TEAMWORK

As team leader and manager in most cases, how you think and act and perform under stress will affect the team performance. If you are in charge of training and supervision of the team, how you listen, how you teach, and how you engage your team will be the key to teamwork.

c. BETTER PRODUCTION

If you don't run your business correctly it will directly effect production. You have to direct your team to develop and execute the systems that lead to efficiency, effective scheduling and time management.

d. BETTER TEAM COMMUNICATION

As the leader of your team, you have to be mature enough to lead all communications, and to teach your team to communicate better by setting the example by being transparent and honest in all your dealings with your team. Part of that is to admit when you make a mistake and apologize when you get out of line. This will create a safe environment for the team so that they can bring up and discuss problems when they arise. Quite often, you will have blind spots in your point of view and if you are open to listen to your team, you will end up with a wider perspective and a more productive team.

e. BETTER TRUST

Trust is the base of the pyramid that great teamwork is built upon. Without trust from the team, you will never have a good team. This is not something that is built in a day, but it starts with communications, working through one issue after another until there is a base to build on.

f. BETTER PRODUCTIVE CONFLICT RESOLUTION

Once trust is built you can work on the ability to discuss sensitive issues in order to take the next step in building a great team. Conflict will happen; there is no way to avoid it. When you have three or five or ten different people working in a close, high-energy environment, there is always conflict.

You have patients come in every day that create tension and conflict. They have their agenda and want you to fix the problem right now. There are skills and exercises you can learn to help you practice resolving conflict. This too, takes time.

You can't just read this book and learn to do that. It takes a real commitment. If you don't learn to overcome this hurdle, you will never resolve the day-to-day issues and will halt any progress you have made with team building. You are the leader of the team, so you need to learn to face this issue first and then lead the team to learn too.

g. BETTER TEAM BUY-IN

Team building and harvesting the benefits of higher EQ happen when the team learns to communicate, then builds trust and finally learns to manage conflict. After these steps are complete, the result is that the team will begin to buy-in to the vision you have for the team, the way you want to practice, the things that will increase production and create a more enjoyable atmosphere. They will pitch in and help each other more, and will understand why you want them to do the things you ask them to do. They will own the team themselves and become more self-motivated. This is when working with your team will become fun.

h. BETTER TEAM ACCOUNTABILITY

Once the team buys-in, they will start being more accountable. They will become more self-directed, but the most important part is that they will become accountable, not only to you but to each other. They will expect help when they need it, they will pitch in, in areas they are not the primarily responsible person for the job. They will be interested in daily production, and know that if they are more productive, it helps the team, the bottom line, and ultimately themselves. This is a picture of a group that has improved their Emotional Intelligence, and realize that the greater good of the team is also good for themselves.

i. BETTER TEAM COOPERATION

Emotionally Intelligent people understand cooperation, for all the reasons listed above. Getting along with people that you see more than you see your family is useful and smart. It lessens their stress and makes for a much happier life.

THE LAST WORD

I believe that improving your Emotional Intelligence is the one factor that separates good dentists from exceptional dentists. I am sure you can look around and see the rock stars in your own town or in the dental society—they have that something special, something different that sets them apart.

You may have trained at the same school, gone to the same continuing education courses, and done the same type services. I know I have met some of the leading dentists in the nation when I went to the AACD and other national courses like the Pankey Institute. I thought to myself, "why is this person speaking and lecturing and showing these huge cases that I never seem to find?"

Some of that is their persona, some people can just walk into the room and immediately all eyes are turned on him or her. They have that engaging personality, sort of like Tony Robbins or Zig Ziegler. They take charge of the room. Those people are rare and exceptional.

I have met people who have incredible clinical skills and are great teachers. They have a talent that draws people to them because of the reputation they have built in the dental community. I think this is the group that has learned Emotional Intelligence, whether by accident or by purpose and intent. When they increase their EQ, they will understand about talking to people to identify their needs and giving them what they want. I also think this group has become skilled in knowing how to handle their team and their patients because they have those interpersonal skills. This leads to better patient selection, better scheduling and better case acceptance. With this maturity, they learn how to market to the people they want to treat.

Yes, having superb clinical and technical skills is essential to having a great practice.

Yes, having the cognitive ability to make great diagnostic decisions and run their business in a proper way is essential to having a good practice.

And YES, I do believe the secret to exceptional success is developing their Emotional Intelligence so that they understand themselves and all the people around them. They will be able to act in a way that they can have empathy and understanding for others and manage their relationships in a way that creates success. They also have an unusual level of commitment. They listen, they learn, they understand, and they love dentistry. They also will work their tail off to do things other people will not do.

It is Simple, but it is not Easy. It is worth the Effort to become more EMOTIONALLY INTELLIGENT!

BIBLIOGRAPHY

I was deeply influenced by reading several books about dentistry, but more about Emotional Intelligence. I acknowledge that I used information gained by reading each of these books. I applied this knowledge to how it pertained to the practice of dentistry and having a better, more fulfilling life by use of this information.

Emotional Intelligence, Daniel Goleman, Bantam Books, Tenth Anniversary Edition, 2006.

The Emotional Intelligence Activity Kit, Adele B. Lynn & Janele R Lynn, Audibles.com

The Power of Purpose, Richard J. Leider, 3rd Edition, Berrett-Koehler Publishers, Inc. 2015

Leadership, The Power of Emotional Intelligence, Daniel Goleman, Selected Writings, More than Sound, LLC, 2011

50 Activities for Developing Emotional Intelligence, Adele B. Lynn, HRD Press, Inc, 2000

Essentialism, Greg McKeown, Crown Publishing Group, 2014

Key Takeaways, Analysis & Review of Tom Rath's Strengthfinder 2.0, Eureka Books

Primal Leadership, Daniel Goleman, Richard Boyatzis, Annie McKee, Harvard Business Review Press, 2013

Making it Easy for Patients to Say "Yes", Paul Homoly, 2005

Generational Selling Tactics that Work, Cam Marston, John Willey & Sons, Inc., 2011

Emotional Intelligence, 100+ Skills, Tips, Tricks & Techniques to Improve Interpersonal Connection, Control Your Emotions, Build Self-Confidence & Find Long Lasting Success!, Kevin Moore, 2016

HRB'S 10 Best Reads, On Emotional Intelligence, 2015

Start with WHY, Simon Sinek, Penguin Group, 2009

Sales EQ, Jeb Blount, John Wiley & Sons, 2017

Overcoming the Five Dysfunctions of a Team, Patrick Lencioni, Jossey-Bass, 2005

Everything DiSC Manual, Mark Scullard, Dabney Baum, John Wiley & Sons, 2015